John Kember and Catherine Ramsden

Flute Sight-Reading 2

Déchiffrage pour la flûte 2
Vom-Blatt-Spiel auf der Flöte 2

A fresh approach / Nouvelle approche
Eine erfrischend neue Methode

ED12818
ISMN M-2201-2379-5

SCHOTT

Mainz · London · Madrid · New York · Paris · Prague · Tokyo · Toronto
© 2006 Schott Music Ltd, London · Printed in Germany

ED 12818

British Library Cataloguing-in-Publication Data.
A catalogue record for this book is available from the British Library
ISMN M-2201-2379-5
ISBN 1-902455-51-7

French translation: Agnès Ausseur
German translation: Ute Corleis
Cover design and layout by www.adamhaystudio.com
Music setting and page layout by Jackie Leigh
Printed in Germany S&Co.8041

Contents
Sommaire/Inhalt

Preface

Flute Sight-Reading 2 aims to build on the sight-reading skills learnt in book 1 and provides a wealth of more challenging examples so that the pupil may gain even greater confidence when approaching any new piece of music for the first time. There are five sections, each of which gradually introduces new notes, rhythms, articulations, dynamics, ornaments and Italian terms in a logical sequence, much as you would find in a flute tutor. The emphasis is on providing idiomatic tunes and structures rather than sterile sight-reading exercises.

Each section begins with several solo examples and concludes with duets and accompanied pieces, enabling the player to gain experience of sight-reading within the context of ensemble playing. The reader will still be urged to consider each piece initially for its rhythmic content, but with the added awareness of tempo and style. Students are encouraged to perform each piece in the manner of style indicated and to play not only fluently but also musically and expressively: an interesting and musically shaped performance is always preferable to one that is technically correct but dull.

Section 1 uses a two-octave range, from low C to high C. Both simple and compound times are used and there are some changes of time signature within individual pieces.

Section 2 extends the range to high D and includes some off-beat quavers, triplets and semiquaver rests. It also introduces another sight-reading challenge: the Da Capo and Dal Segno al Fine.

Section 3 extends the range to high F. Swing rhythms are encountered for the first time and the double sharp is introduced.

Section 4 extends the range to high G and introduces ornaments: the appoggiatura and the acciaccatura. There is an increased use of chromatic patterns, which means there are many more accidentals in this section.

Section 5 makes use of more ornaments: the mordent, turn and trill. All the keys with up to four sharps or flats are revised, and modes, whole-tone scales and the pentatonic scale are introduced.

To the pupil

The object of these pieces is to encourage the habit of sight-reading, both in solo form and in duets and accompanied pieces, in order to prepare you for reading in both solo and ensemble situations.

It is always recommended that your first consideration should be to realise the overall style of each piece and to establish a pulse in your mind before you begin to play. This can be achieved very quickly with practice.

Be constantly aware of the key and accidentals required in each piece and always look out for changes that may occur in both the accidentals and the time signatures.

Above all, aim always to **play musically** by creating shape as indicated by the dynamics and phrasing. Call on your experience to give a stylistic, expressive and musical interpretation at all times.

Reading at sight is an essential 'life' skill for all musicians. It gives you the **independence** to explore **your choice** of music for yourself, drawing material from either the past or today's popular repertoire.

> **Always** be careful to observe time and key signatures.
> **Always** consider the rhythm first.
> **Always** aim to maintain continuity and pulse.
> And, above all, **always** attempt to play musically.

Be independent: be free to choose, explore and enjoy!

Préface

Déchiffrage pour la flûte 2 s'appuie sur les aptitudes de lecture à vue acquises dans le volume 1 et présente une foison de configurations plus exigeantes qui renforceront l'assurance de l'élève lors de sa première approche d'une pièce de musique. Ce volume, divisé en cinq sections, introduit progressivement notes, rythmes, phrasés, nuances, ornements et termes italiens nouveaux selon un ordre logique respectant celui d'une méthode de flûte. Le propos est ici d'offrir des morceaux de musique et des structures caractéristiques du jeu de la flûte de préférence à de stériles exercices de déchiffrage.

Chaque section débute par plusieurs pièces en solo et se termine par des duos et des pièces accompagnées qui familiariseront avec le déchiffrage dans le cadre de l'exécution collective. Comme dans le volume précédent, le lecteur est fortement incité à envisager d'abord le contenu rythmique de chaque pièce mais avec un sens accru du tempo et du style. Les instrumentistes sont encouragés à respecter le style indiqué pour chaque morceau et à jouer non seulement avec aisance mais aussi avec musicalité et expression : une interprétation construite et musicale sera toujours préférable à une exécution techniquement correcte mais sans relief.

La section 1 se déploie sur deux octaves, du *do* grave au *do* aigu, et comporte des mesures simples et des mesures composées, ainsi que des changements de mesure en cours d'exécution.

La section 2 prolonge l'étendue de jeu jusqu'au *ré* aigu et inclut des croches, des triolets et des quarts de soupirs à contretemps. Deux nouvelles composantes du déchiffrage y sont abordées : le *Da capo* et le *Dal segno al fine*.

La section 3 prolonge l'étendue de jeu jusqu'au *fa* aigu. Des rythmes *swing* y apparaissent ainsi que le double dièse.

La section 4 prolonge l'étendue de jeu jusqu'au *sol* aigu et introduit les ornements de l'*appogiatura* et l'*acciaccatura*. Le recours aux formules chromatiques y est de plus en plus fréquent et, par conséquent, les altérations accidentelles y sont beaucoup plus nombreuses.

La section 5 introduit les nouveaux ornements du mordant, du *gruppetto* et du trille. Toutes les tonalités comportant jusqu'à quatre altérations à la clef y sont revues et les modes, les gammes par tons et la gamme pentatonique y sont abordés.

A l'élève

Le propos de ces morceaux est d'encourager l'habitude du déchiffrage en solo, en duo ou accompagné au piano, de manière à préparer à la lecture à vue soliste ou collective.

Il est recommandé de toujours envisager en premier lieu le style général de chaque pièce et d'établir une pulsation intérieure avant de commencer à jouer. Ceci s'acquiert très rapidement avec de l'entraînement.

Soyez constamment conscient de la tonalité de chaque pièce et des altérations qui y sont nécessaires tout en demeurant sans cesse attentif aux altérations accidentelles et aux changements de mesure qui peuvent survenir.

Avant tout, efforcez-vous de jouer **avec musicalité** en donnant le relief indiqué par les nuances et le phrasé. Appuyez-vous sur votre expérience pour donner à tout moment une interprétation stylée, expressive et musicale.

La lecture à vue est essentielle à la « survie » de tout musicien. Elle procure une **indépendance** permettant l'exploration par vous-même de la musique de **votre choix**, du répertoire passé ou contemporain.

> **Toujours** repérer les indications de mesure et de tonalité.
> **Toujours** envisager le rythme en premier lieu.
> **Toujours** s'efforcer de maintenir continuité et pulsation.
> **Toujours**, et surtout, jouer avec musicalité.

L'indépendance procure la liberté de choisir, d'explorer et de se faire plaisir !

Vorwort

Vom-Blatt-Spiel auf der Flöte 2 baut auf den Fähigkeiten auf, die in Buch 1 erworben wurden, und stellt eine Fundgrube mit anspruchsvolleren Beispielen dar, so dass der Schüler mit noch mehr Selbstvertrauen an die Erarbeitung eines neuen Musikstücks herangehen wird. Es gibt fünf Teile, von denen jeder allmählich neue Noten, Rhythmen, Artikulation, Dynamik, Verzierungen und italienische Begriffe in einer logischen Abfolge einführt. Also ganz ähnlich, wie es ein Flötenlehrer auch machen würde. Der Schwerpunkt liegt auf idiomatischen Melodien und Strukturen statt sterilen Blatt-Spiel Übungen.

Jeder Teil beginnt mit mehreren Solobeispielen und endet mit Duetten und begleiteten Stücken. Dadurch kann der Spieler auch Erfahrungen im Blatt-Spiel beim gemeinsamen Musizieren mit anderen machen. Auch in diesem Band wird der Leser dazu aufgefordert, jedes Stück erst einmal auf seinen rhythmischen Gehalt hin zu betrachten, aber mit dem zusätzlichen Bewusstsein für Tempo und Stil. Die Schüler werden dazu ermutigt, jedes Stück in der angegebenen Stilart wiederzugeben, und dabei nicht nur flüssig, sondern auch musikalisch und ausdrucksvoll zu spielen: eine interessante und musikalische Darbietung ist grundsätzlich einer technisch korrekten, aber langweiligen vorzuziehen.

Teil 1 benutzt einen Umfang von zwei Oktaven, vom c^1 bis zum c^3. Es kommen sowohl einfache als auch zusammengesetzte Taktarten vor, und innerhalb einiger Stücke kommt es zu Taktwechseln.

Teil 2 erweitert den Umfang bis zum d^3 und schließt einige Achtel auf unbetonten Zählzeiten, Triolen und Sechzehntelpausen mit ein. Außerdem wird eine weitere Herausforderung des Vom-Blatt-Spiels vorgestellt: die Zeichen *Da Capo* und *Dal Segno al Fine*.

Teil 3 erweitert den Umfang bis zum f^3. Zum ersten Mal begegnet man Swing-Rhythmen und das Doppelkreuz wird eingeführt.

Teil 4 erweitert den Umfang bis zum g^3 und stellt Verzierungen vor: *Appoggiatura* und *Acciaccatura*. Zunehmend werden chromatische Muster benutzt, was bedeutet, dass es in diesem Teil sehr viel mehr Vorzeichen gibt.

Teil 5 benutzt noch mehr Verzierungen: Mordent, Doppelschlag und Triller. Alle Tonarten bis zu vier Kreuz- und B-Tonarten werden wiederholt, und Kirchentonarten, Ganztonleitern und die pentatonische Tonleiter werden eingeführt.

An den Schüler

Ziel ist es, mit diesen Stücken die Gewohnheit des Vom-Blatt-Spiels weiter zu festigen. Das soll sowohl mit solistischen Stücken als auch mit Duetten und begleiteten Stücken geschehen. Dadurch wirst du darauf vorbereitet, sowohl in Solo- als auch in kammermusikalischen Situationen vom Blatt zu lesen.

Dein erstes Augenmerk sollte immer dem Erkennen des vorherrschenden Stils in jedem Stückes gelten sowie der Verankerung eines Pulsschlages in deinem Kopf. Erst dann beginne zu spielen. Mit ein bisschen Übung kann das sehr schnell erreicht werden.

Sei dir immer der Tonart und den Vorzeichen, die in jedem Stück gebraucht werden, bewusst. Achte immer auf Veränderungen, die sowohl bei den Vorzeichen als auch bei den Taktarten vorkommen können.

Dein oberstes Ziel sollte es immer sein, **musikalisch zu spielen**, indem man die Form herausarbeitet, die durch Dynamik und Phrasierung angezeigt wird. Greife auf deine Erfahrung zurück, um jederzeit eine stilistische, ausdrucksstarke und musikalische Interpretation darzubieten.

Vom-Blatt Spielen ist eine wesentliche ‚Lebens'-Fähigkeit für alle Musiker. Sie bietet dir die **Unabhängigkeit**, deine **Musikauswahl** selbst zu treffen, wobei entweder Material aus der Vergangenheit oder aus dem heutzutage beliebten Repertoire herangezogen wird.

> Bestimme **immer** sehr sorgfältig Takt- und Tonart.
> Bedenke **immer** zuerst den Rhythmus.
> Setze dir zum Ziel, **immer** die Kontinuität und den Pulsschlag beizubehalten.
> Und vor allem anderen: versuche **immer**, musikalisch zu spielen.

Sei unabhängig: fühle dich frei, zu wählen, zu entdecken und zu genießen!

* This page is left blank to save
an unnecessary page turn later.

* Feuillet laissé blanc pour faciliter
la bonne tourne des pages.

* Aus wendetechnischen Gründen
bleibt diese Seite frei.

Section 1 – Two-octave range; changes of time signature within pieces

Section 1 – Tessiture de deux octaves ; changements de mesure à l'intérieur d'une pièce

Teil 1 – Umfang von zwei Oktaven; Taktwechsel innerhalb einiger Stücke

Reading at sight: giving a musical performance

1. Look at the **time signature** and check for any changes within the piece. Tap the rhythm, feeling the pulse throughout. Count at least one bar in your head before you begin to play.

2. Look at the **key signature**. Identify which notes (if any!) the sharps and flats apply to. Also look for **accidentals** in the piece.

3. Look for **patterns**. While tapping the rhythm, look at the melodic shape and notice movement by step, skip, repeated notes and sequence.

4. Observe the **articulations** and **dynamics**.

5. Above all, make a **musical performance** of each piece. Before you begin, observe the character of the music given in the performance direction, keep looking ahead whilst playing and, above all, keep going.

La lecture à vue est d'abord une exécution musicale

1. Vérifiez l'**indication de mesure** et recherchez les changements se produisant au cours de la pièce. Frappez le rythme en maintenant une pulsation intérieure constante. Comptez au moins une mesure mentalement avant de commencer à jouer.

2. Vérifiez l'**indication de la tonalité**. Repérez à quelles notes s'appliquent les altérations. Recherchez également les **altérations accidentelles**.

3. Repérez les **motifs**. Tout en frappant le rythme, observez les contours mélodiques et les déplacements par degré, les sauts d'intervalles, les notes répétées et les séquences.

4. Examiner les **phrasés** et les **nuances dynamiques**.

5. Avant tout, donnez une **exécution musicale** de chaque morceau. Avant de commencer, cernez le caractère de la musique à l'aide des indications d'exécution, lisez à l'avance pendant que vous jouez et, surtout, ne vous arrêtez pas.

Vom Blatt lesen: eine musikalische Vorstellung geben

1. Schaue dir die **Taktart** genau an und überprüfe das ganze Stück auf eventuelle Taktänderungen. Schlage den Rhythmus und fühle durchweg den Pulsschlag. Zähle mindestens einen Takt im Kopf vor, bevor du zu spielen beginnst.

2. Jetzt schaue auf die **Tonart**. Suche die Noten heraus (wenn es überhaupt welche gibt!), zu denen die Kreuz- und B-Vorzeichen gehören. Achte auch auf **Vorzeichen** innerhalb des Stückes.

3. Achte auf **Muster**. Betrachte die melodische Form, während du den Rhythmus schlägst, und erkenne Schritt- und Sprungbewegungen sowie sich wiederholende Noten und Sequenzen.

4. Nun studiere **Artikulation** und **Dynamik**.

5. Am allerwichtigsten ist: mache aus jedem Stück eine **musikalische Darbietung**. Bevor du anfängst, schaue dir noch den Charakter der Musik, der sich in den Vortragsangaben widerspiegelt, genau an, schaue beim Spielen immer nach vorne und, vor allem, spiele immer weiter.

Glossary of terms

Adagio	slow
Allegro	quick
Andante	at a walking pace
Andantino	slightly faster than Andante
Animato	animated, lively
Appassionato	with passion
Cantabile	in a singing style
Con brio	with vigour
Con grazia	gracefully
Con moto	with movement
Crescendo (*cresc.*)	gradually getting louder
Diminuendo (*dim.*)	gradually getting softer
Dolce	sweetly
Espressivo (*espress.*)	expressively
Gigue	a dance in 6/8 time
Giocoso	playful, humorous
Legato	smoothly
Leggiero	light
Lento	slow
Marcato	emphatic
Mesto	sad
Moderato	at a moderate speed
Molto	much
Non	not
Poco	little
Presto	fast
Rallentando (rall.)	gradually getting slower
Ritardando (rit.)	getting slower
Ritmico	rhythmically
Scherzando	playful, joking
Sempre	always
Simile (*sim.*)	continue in the same way
Subito	suddenly
Tempo primo	first speed
Troppo	too much
Valse	waltz
Veloce	swift
Vivace	lively

Glossaire

Adagio	lent
Allegro	rapide
Andante	allant
Andantino	un peu plus vite qu'*andante*
Animato	animé
Appassionato	passionné
Cantabile	chantant
Con brio	avec éclat
Con grazia	avec grâce
Con moto	avec mouvement
Crescendo (*cresc.*)	de plus en plus fort
Diminuendo (*dim.*)	de plus en plus doux
Dolce	doux
Espressivo (*espress.*)	expressif
Gigue	danse à 6/8
Giocoso	joyeux
Legato	lié
Leggiero	léger
Lento	lent
Marcato	marqué
Mesto	triste
Moderato	modéré
Molto	Très
Non	non, pas
Poco	peu
Presto	rapide
Rallentando (rall.)	en ralentissant
Ritardando (rit.)	en retardant
Ritmico	rythmé
Scherzando	en badinant
Sempre	toujours
Simile (*sim.*)	de la même façon
Subito	soudain
Tempo primo	au premier mouvement
Troppo	trop
Valse	danse à 3 temps
Veloce	véloce
Vivace	vif

Glossar

Adagio	langsam
Allegro	schnell
Andante	gehend
Andantino	etwas schneller als Andante
Animato	lebendig, lebhaft
Appassionato	mit Leidenschaft
Cantabile	sanglich
Con brio	mit Feuer
Con grazia	anmutig
Con moto	mit Bewegung
Crescendo (*cresc.*)	allmählich lauter werdend
Diminuendo (*dim.*)	allmählich leiser werdend
Dolce	süß
Espressivo (*espress.*)	ausdrucksvoll
Gigue	ein Tanz im 6/8-Takt
Giocoso	spielerisch, humorvoll
Legato	gebunden
Leggiero	leicht
Lento	langsam
Marcato	betont
Mesto	traurig
Moderato	gemäßigt
Molto	viel
Non	nicht
Poco	wenig
Presto	schnell
Rallentando (rall.)	allmählich langsamer werdend
Ritardando (rit.)	langsamer werdend
Ritmico	rhythmisch
Scherzando	spielerisch, scherzend
Sempre	immer
Simile (*sim.*)	auf gleiche Weise
Subito	plötzlich
Tempo primo	das Tempo vom Anfang
Troppo	zuviel
Valse	Walzer
Veloce	schnell
Vivace	lebhaft

Section 1 – Two-octave range; changes of time signature within pieces

Section 1 – Tessiture de deux octaves ; changements de mesure à l'intérieur d'une pièce

Teil 1 – Umfang von zwei Oktaven; Taktwechsel innerhalb einiger Stücke

3.

Valse

mp cantabile

cresc.

f

4.

Scherzando

mf

5.

Vivace

mf

cresc.

mp

dim.

12

6.

Marcato

dim.   f

mp   molto rit. e dim.

7.

Animato

f

p

mf cresc.

f   f cresc.

This piece begins on the second beat of the bar in 3-time. Count 1 2 3 1 before you begin.

Cette pièce commence sur le deuxième temps d'une mesure à 3 temps. Comptez 1, 2, 3, 1 avant d'attaquer.

Dieses Stück beginnt auf dem zweiten Schlag des 3/8-Taktes. Zähle 1 2 3 1, bevor du beginnst.

F#minor: look out for the E#s.   En *fa*# mineur : attention aux *mi*#.   Fis-Moll: Achte auf das Eis.

10.

Andante moderato

11.

Moderato

12.

Andante, legato e dolce

13.

Adagio non troppo

mp espress.

14.

Ritmico

f

mf

15.

Vivace

mf

f

poco dim.

16.

Andantino

mp espress.　　　　　　　　　　　　　　　　　　　*cresc. poco a poco*

f　　　*dim.*

sempre dim.

17.

Con brio

f

subito p

mf　　　　　　　　*molto cresc.*　　　*ff*

18.

Con grazia

mp dolce espress.

sempre dim. *pp*

19.

Allegro molto

20.

Poco lento

p legato

21.

22.

Andante mesto

mp

legato

sim.

23.

24.

Dolce e legato

poco animato

rall. . . . . . a tempo

25.

26.

27.

28.

Molto appassionato

Section 2 – Extending the range to high D; triplets, off-beat quavers and semiquaver rests

Section 2 – Extension de la tessiture au *ré* aigu ; triolets, croches à contretemps et quarts de soupir

Teil 2 – Ausdehnung des Umfangs bis zum d³; Achtelnoten auf unbetonte Zählzeiten, Triolen und Sechzehntelpausen

Reading at sight: giving a musical performance

Firstly, identify the **character** of the piece – fast, slow, happy, march etc.

Observe all the **details** within the piece: **dynamics, articulations, accidentals,** any **other instructions** and, of course, the **time signature** and **key signature.**

Choose an **appropriate speed** both for the piece and for yourself – ensure you are going to be comfortable enough to make a musical and technically-accurate performance at the first attempt. Count at least a bar before you begin to play so as to secure the right speed.

While playing, always **look ahead** so you have time to prepare for what is coming. In addition to playing the **right notes** with **rhythmic accuracy,** keep paying attention to all the **details** as they occur: slurs and tongued notes, staccatos, dynamics, and any other instructions in the score.

Glossary of terms
Alla marcia   in the style of a March
Misterioso   mysteriously
Niente   nothing
Semplice   simple, plain
Vivo   lively, quick
Da Capo (D.C.) from the beginning
Dal Segno (D.S.)   from the sign 𝄋
Fine   the end of the piece

La lecture à vue est d'abord une exécution musicale

Cernez, tout d'abord, le **caractère** du morceau : rapide, lent, joyeux, marche, etc.

Examinez touts les **détails** contenus dans le morceau : **nuances, phrasés, altérations accidentelles,** toutes les autres **indications** et, bien sûr, celles de **mesure** et de **tonalité.**

Etablissez un **mouvement convenable** à la fois pour la pièce et pour vous-même. Assurez-vous d'être assez à l'aise pour donner une exécution musicale et techniquement exacte au premier essai. Comptez au moins une mesure avant de commencer à jouer de manière à prendre la bonne vitesse.

Pendant que vous jouez, lisez toujours **à l'avance** afin d'avoir le temps de vous préparer à ce qui vient. Tout en exécutant les **notes justes** avec **exactitude rythmique,** ne relâchez pas votre attention aux détails au fur et à mesure de leur apparition : liaisons et coups de langue, staccatos, nuances et autres indications portées sur la partition.

Glossaire
Alla marcia   en style de marche
Misterioso   mystérieux
Niente   rien
Semplice   simple
Vivo   vif
Da Capo (D.C.)   du début
Dal Segno (D.S.)   du signe 𝄋
Fine   fin

Vom Blatt lesen: eine musikalische Vorstellung geben

Identifiziere als erstes den **Charakter** des Stückes – schnell, langsam, glücklich, marschartig, etc.

Achte auf alle **Details** innerhalb des Stückes: **Dynamik, Artikulation, Vorzeichen,** alle **anderen Anweisungen** und natürlich die **Takt- und Tonart.**

Wähle ein **geeignetes Tempo,** das sowohl dem Stück als auch deinem Können gerecht wird – versichere dich, dass du dich wohl genug fühlst, um gleich beim ersten Versuch eine musikalische und technisch genaue Vorstellung zu geben. Um das richtige Tempo zu verankern, zähle mindestens einen Takt im Kopf vor, bevor du zu spielen beginnst.

Schaue beim Spielen **immer voraus,** damit du genügend Zeit hast, um dich auf das Kommende vorzubereiten. Achte zusätzlich zum Spielen der **richtigen Noten** mit **rhythmischer Genauigkeit** auf alle **Details,** wenn sie auftauchen: Bindungen und gestoßene Noten, Stakkato, Dynamik und alle anderen Anweisungen in der Notenstimme.

Glossar
Alla marcia   im Stile eines Marsches
Misterioso   geheimnisvoll
Niente   nichts
Semplice   einfach, klar
Vivo   lebhaft, schnell
Da Capo (D.C.)   vom Anfang
Dal Segno (D.S.)   ab Zeichen 𝄋
Fine   das Ende des Stückes

Section 2 – Extending the range to high D; triplets, off-beat quavers and semiquaver rests

Section 2 – Extension de la tessiture au *ré* aigu ; triolets, croches à contretemps et quarts de soupir

Teil 2 – Ausdehnung des Umfangs bis zum d³; Achtelnoten auf unbetonte Zählzeiten, Triolen und Sechzehntelpausen

29.

30.

31.

32.

33.

Alla marcia

34.

Moderato

35.

Vivace

36.

37.

38.

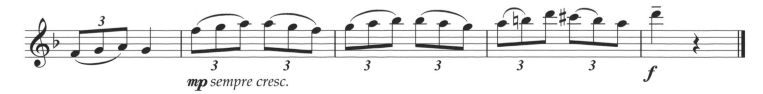

39.

Ragtime

40.

Moderato

41.

Habanera

Fine

D.C. al Fine

42.

(Aeolian mode) (Mode éolien) (Äolisch)

43.

44.

45.

46.

47.

48.

Giocoso

49.

Andantino

rall. e dim.

50.

51.

52.

53.

Habanera

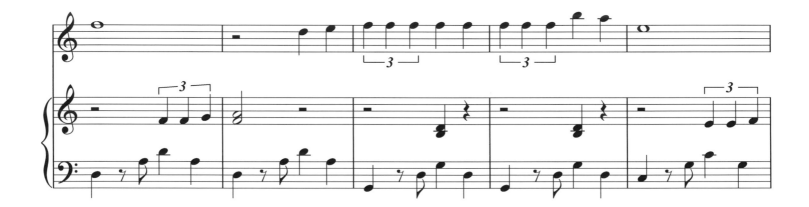

54.

38

55.

56.

Semplice e espressivo

57.

Moderate waltz tempo

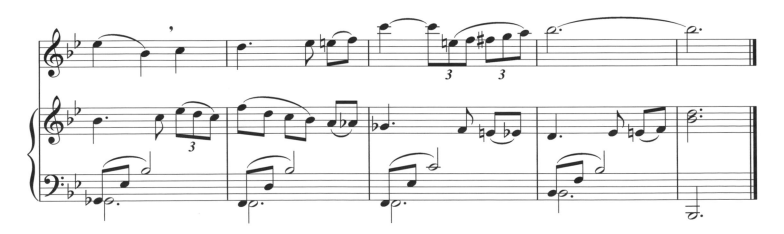

Section 3 – Extending the range to high F; swing rhythms; 5/8, 7/8 and 8/8

Section 3 – Extension de la tessiture au *fa* aigu ; rythme *swing* ; mesures à 5/8, 7/8 et 8/8

Teil 3 – Erweiterung des Umfangs bis zum f³; Swing-Rhythmen und neue Taktarten: 5/8, 7/8 und 8/8

Swing Rhythm

Swing rhythm is what most people think of as 'Jazz', with its easily-recognizable relaxed triplet feel. The swing era began in the 1940s and 50s, with the Big Bands of Glenn Miller, Benny Goodman and Count Basie, and the singers Nat King Cole and Ella Fitzgerald. Quavers (eighth-notes) take on a loose

 feel,

though they are generally written as

The Double Sharp

Piece 62 contains the note 'F double sharp', notated

A **single** sharp raises the note by **one** semitone; a **double** sharp raises the note by **two** semitones.

The double flat, notated ,

works in exactly the same way, lowering the note by two semitones.

Rythme *swing*

Le rythme *swing* est associé la plupart de temps au Jazz et se reconnaît facilement à sa pulsation libre de triolet. L'ère du *swing* commença dans les années 1940 et 1950, avec les *Big Bands* de Glenn Miller, de Benny Goodman et de Count Basie, et avec les chanteurs Nat King Cole et Ella Fitzgerald. Les croches y adoptent une allure plus dégagée,

quoique généralement notées ainsi :

Le double dièse

Le morceau n° 62 contient la note *fa* double dièse notée

Le dièse élève la note d'**un** demi-ton, le **double** dièse élève la note de **deux** demi-tons.

Le double bémol

agit exactement de la même façon en abaissant la note de deux demi-tons.

Der Swingrhythmus

Die meisten Leute verbinden mit dem Swingrhythmus den ‚Jazz' mit seinem leicht erkennbaren, entspannten Triolengefühl. Die Swingära begann in den 40er- und 50er-Jahren mit den Big Bands von Glenn Miller, Benny Goodman und Count Basie, sowie den Sängern Nat King Cole und Ella Fitzgerald. Die Achtelnoten werden ab jener Zeit lockerer gespielt,

obwohl sie grundsätzlich als

geschrieben werden.

Das Doppelkreuz

Stück Nr. 62 beinhaltet die Note fisis, die folgendermaßen notiert wird:

Ein **einzelnes** Kreuz erhöht die Note um **einen** Halbton; ein **Doppelkreuz** erhöht die Note um **zwei** Halbtöne.

Das Doppel-B, das

geschrieben wird, funktioniert auf genau die gleiche Art und Weise, wobei die Note um zwei Halbtöne erniedrigt wird.

Glossary of terms

Amabile	pleasantly
Brillante	brilliant
Capriccioso	
	in a whimsical, fanciful style
Dolente	sad, mournful
Doloroso	sad, mournful
Energico	energetically
Grazioso	gracefully
Nobilmente	nobly
Pesante	heavy
Piacevole	pleasant
Sostenuto	sustained
Spiritoso	spirited
Tristamente	sadly
Vif	lively
Vigoroso	vigorous, strong

Glossaire

Amabile	aimable
Brillante	brillant
Capriccioso	capricieux
Dolente	affligé
Doloroso	douloureux
Energico	énergique
Grazioso	gracieux
Nobilmente	avec noblesse
Pesante	lourd
Piacevole	plaisant
Sostenuto	soutenu
Spiritoso	avec esprit
Tristamente	tristement
Vif	(vif)
Vigoroso	vigoureux

Glossar

Amabile	liebenswürdig
Brillante	brilliant
Capriccioso	launisch, eigenwillig
Dolente	traurig, trauernd
Doloroso	traurig, trauernd
Energico	energisch
Grazioso	anmutig
Nobilmente	edel
Pesante	schwer
Piacevole	gefällig
Sostenuto	zurückhaltend
Spiritoso	geistvoll
Tristamente	traurig
Vif	lebendig
Vigoroso	kräftig, stark

Section 3 – Extending the range to high F; swing rhythms; 5/8, 7/8 and 8/8

Section 3 – Extension de la tessiture au *fa* aigu ; rythme *swing* ; mesures à 5/8, 7/8 et 8/8

Teil 3 – Erweiterung des Umfangs bis zum f³; Swing-Rhythmen und neue Taktarten: 5/8, 7/8 und 8/8

58.

59.

60.

Giocoso

61.

Spiritoso

62.

Capriccioso

63.

Brilliante

64.

Nobilmente

65.

Tristamente

66.

Moderato

67.

Allegretto

senza rit.

68.

Doloroso

69.

Dolente

70.

Vigoroso

71.

Medium swing

72.

Medium swing

73.

Medium swing

74.

Note: Where breath marks are in different places ensure that quick breaths are taken to avoid interrupting the flow.

N.B. Si les indications de respiration sont placées différemment, assurez-vous de prendre des inspirations rapides pour éviter d'interrompre le souffle.

Beachte: Wo an unterschiedlichen Stellen Atemzeichen stehen, musst du schnelle Atemzüge nehmen, um zu vermeiden, dass der Melodiefluss unterbrochen wird.

75.

76.

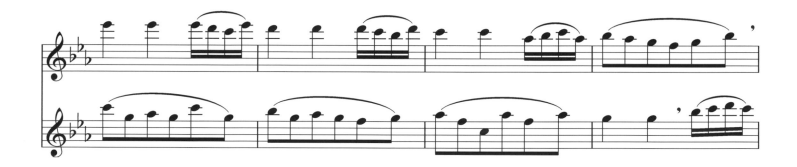

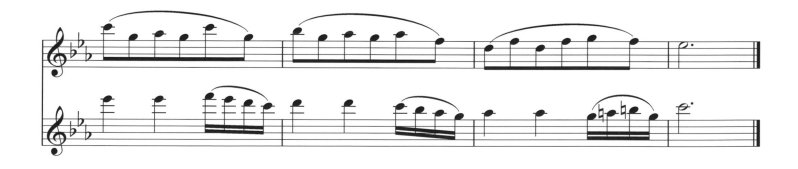

77.

78.

Piacevole

79.

80.

Calypso

81.

Slow swing

82.

Slow blues

83.

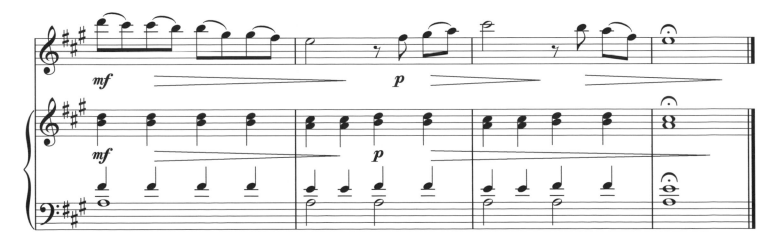

84.

85.

86.

Section 4 – Extending the range to high G; ornamentation; chromatic patterns

Section 4 – Extension de l'étendue de jeu au *sol* aigu ; ornementation ; mouvements chromatiques

Teil 4 – *Erweiterung des Umfangs bis zum g^3; Verzierungen; chromatische Muster*

Ornamentation in music

Acciaccatura (from the Italian *Acciaccàre*, meaning 'to crush') or 'grace note'.

Notated as a small quaver with a diagonal line through the stem, the acciaccatura is played quickly, 'crushed' against the next note:

Appoggiatura (from the Italian *Appoggiàre*, meaning 'to lean').

Notated as a small quaver, but without the diagonal line, the appoggiatura usually takes half the value of the following note:

So,

would be played

and

would be played

Chromatic patterns
Many of the pieces in this section contain chromatic patterns (parts of scales, ascending or descending in semitones). But beware! In some pieces, such as 88, what looks like a portion of a chromatic scale may contain a mixture of tones and semitones.

Ornementation de la musique

Acciaccatura (de l'italien *acciaccàre* : écraser) ou « broderie ».

Notée comme une croche en petit caractère dont la hampe est traversée d'une ligne diagonale, l'acciacatura se joue vite, « plaquée » contre la note suivante :

Appoggiatura (de l'italien *appogiàre* : pencher).

Notée comme une croche en petit caractère mais sans diagonale traversant la hampe, l'appogiature dure généralement la moitié de la valeur de la note suivante :

Ainsi

s'exécute

et

s'exécute

Mouvements chromatiques
Plusieurs des pièces de cette section contiennent des mouvements chromatiques (fragments de gammes, motifs ascendants ou descendants en demi-tons). Mais attention ! Dans certaines pièces, comme le n° 88, un passage d'allure chromatique peut comporter un mélange de tons et de demi-tons.

Verzierungen in der Musik

Acciaccatura stammt vom italienischen Wort *Acciaccàre*, das ‚quetschen' bedeutet, und ist ein kurzer Vorschlag.

Die Acciaccatura, die als eine kleine Achtelnote mit einer diagonalen Linie quer durch den Notenhals notiert wird, wird schnell gespielt, sozusagen gegen die nächste Note gequetscht:

Appoggiatura stammt vom italienischen Wort *Appoggiàre*, das ‚anlehnen' bedeutet.

Die Appoggiatura, die ebenfalls als kleine Achtelnote notiert wird, aber ohne die diagonale Linie, besitzt normalerweise die Hälfte des Wertes der nachfolgenden Note:

Daher wird

wie folgt gespielt

und

folgendermaßen:

Chromatische Muster
Viele der Stücke in diesem Teil beinhalten chromatische Muster (Teile von Tonleitern, die in Halbtönen auf- und absteigen). Aber Vorsicht! Was in einigen Stücken, wie z. B. in Nr. 88, wie der Teil einer chromatischen Tonleiter aussieht, besteht in Wirklichkeit aus einer Mischung von Ganz- und Halbtönen.

Section 4 – Extending the range to high G; ornamentation; chromatic patterns

Section 4 – Extension de l'étendue de jeu au *sol* aigu ; ornementation ; mouvements chromatiques

Teil 4 – Erweiterung des Umfangs bis zum g³; Verzierungen; chromatische Muster

89.

90.

91.

92.

93.

Giocoso

94.

Ritmico

95.

Capriccioso

96.

Semplice

97.

98.

99.

100.

101.

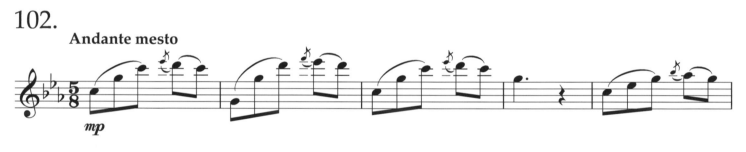

102.

103.

104.

Delicato

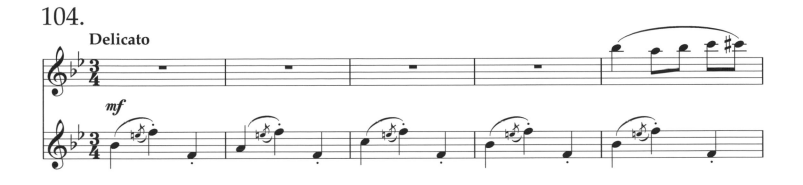

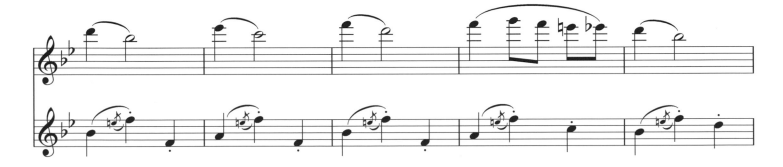

105.

Andantino

106.

Scherzando

107.

Espressivo

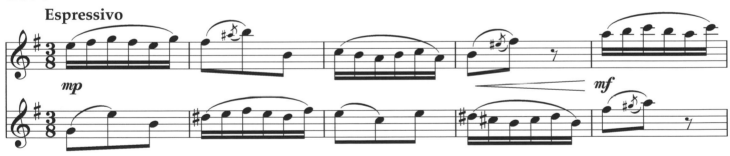

108.

109.

110.

Slow blues feel – medium swing

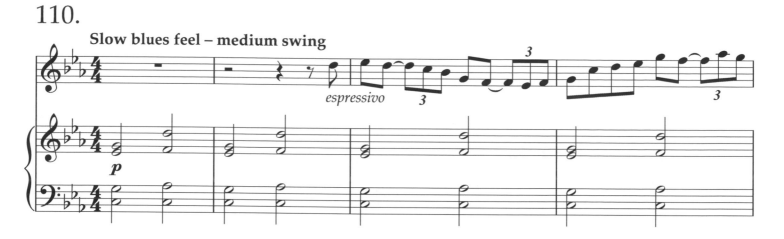

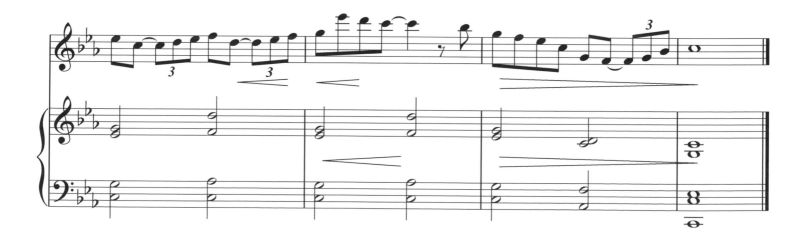

111.

Slow waltz

112.

Section 5 – Revising all previous keys; whole-tone, chromatic and modal patterns; trills, turns and mordents

Section 5 – Révision de toutes les tonalités précédentes ; motifs par tons entiers, chromatismes et modalité ; trilles, *grupetto* et mordants

Teil 5 – Wiederholung aller bisher gelernten Tonarten; Ganzton- und chromatische Muster; Kirchentonarten; Triller, Doppelschläge und Mordente

More ornamentation in music

Turn

The turn is an ornament around a note: up, down and returning to the original note again.

Notated

and played

Notated

and played

Mordent (from the Italian *mòrdere*, meaning to bite).

1. The **Upper Mordent**

is notated

and played

Play the note itself, the note above and back to the original note, as quickly as possible, but retaining clarity.

Nouveaux ornements

Grupetto

Le *grupetto* est un ornement évoluant autour d'une note : au-dessus, au-dessous de la note et revenant à la note originale.

Notation :

exécution :

Notation :

exécution :

Mordant (de l'italien *mòrdere*, mordre).

1. Le **mordant supérieur**,

noté,

s'exécute :

Jouez la note réelle, la note au-dessus d'elle et revenez à la note réelle aussi vite que possible mais avec clarté.

Noch mehr Verzierungen in der Musik

Der Doppelschlag

Der Doppelschlag ist eine Verzierung um die Note herum: auf-, abwärts und wieder zu der Ausgangsnote zurückkehrend.

Notation:

Spielweise:

Notation:

Spielweise:

Der Mordent (vom italienischen Wort *mòrdere*, das ‚beißen' bedeutet).

1. Der ‚obere' Mordent wird

notiert

und

gespielt.

Spiele die Note selbst, dann die darüberliegende Note und wieder die Ausgangsnote so schnell wie möglich, aber ohne an Klarheit zu verlieren.

2. The **Lower Mordent** is notated 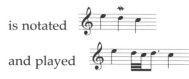 and played

Trill

The trill alternates rapidly between the written note and the note above.

Modes

At the time of the ancient Greeks, musical notes were arranged into modes, and each mode has its own distinct sound and character. Over the centuries the modes changed and developed, and eventually two of them, the Ionian and the Aeolian, became what we now know as the major and minor scale. We can still hear modes in music that is performed today, such as in plainsong (the music of the medieval Church) and in the folk music of many countries.

Pentatonic Scale (from the Greek *Pente*, meaning 'five').

The pentatonic scale consists of just five musical notes (the black notes on the piano) and is commonly found in folk music.

Whole-Tone Scale

The whole-tone scale is made up entirely of notes a whole tone apart. There are only two:

2. **Le mordant inférieur,** noté,  s'exécute :

Trille

Le trille alterne rapidement la note réelle et la note au-dessus d'elle.

Modes

Au temps de l'antiquité grecque, les notes de musique étaient organisées en modes dont chacun possédait une sonorité et un caractère distinctifs. Au cours des siècles, ces modes évoluèrent et se développèrent jusqu'à ce que deux d'entre eux, le mode ionien et le mode éolien, deviennent ce que nous connaissons comme le mode majeur et le mode mineur. On se sert toujours des divers modes aujourd'hui dans certains types de musiques tels que le plain-chant (musique d'église médiévale) et la musique folklorique de nombreuses contrées.

Gamme pentatonique (du grec *pente* : cinq).

La gamme pentatonique n'est composée que de cinq degrés (correspondant aux touches noires du piano) et se rencontre fréquemment dans la musique traditionnelle.

Gamme par tons

La gamme par tons entiers est entièrement composée de degrés séparés d'un ton entre eux. Il n'en n'existe que deux :

2. Der ,**untere' Mordent** wird  notiert und  gespielt.

Der Triller

Der Triller bewegt sich sehr schnell zwischen der geschriebenen und der darüberliegenden Note hin und her.

Die Kirchentonarten

Zur Zeit der alten Griechen wurden die Musiknoten zu Tonarten, den späteren Kirchentonarten, zusammengestellt, von denen jede ihren ganz eigenen Klang und Charakter hat. Über die Jahrhunderte hinweg veränderten und entwickelten sich diese Kirchentonarten. Schließlich wurden zwei von ihnen, Jonisch und Äolisch, das, was heutzutage als Dur- und Moll-Tonleiter bekannt ist. Wir können auch heute noch Kirchentonarten in aufgeführter Musik hören, z. B. im gregorianischen Gesang (der Musik der mittelalterlichen Kirche) und in der Volksmusik vieler Länder.

Die Pentatonik (vom griechischen Wort *Pente*, das ,fünf' bedeutet).

Die pentatonische Tonleiter besteht aus nur fünf Musiknoten (den schwarzen Tasten auf dem Klavier) und ist in der Volksmusik weit verbreitet.

Die Ganztonleiter

Die Ganztonleiter besteht durchweg nur aus Noten, die einen ganzen Ton auseinander stehen. Es gibt insgesamt nur zwei Ganztonleitern:

Section 5 – Revising all previous keys; whole-tone, chromatic and modal patterns; trills, turns and mordents

Section 5 – Révision de toutes les tonalités précédentes ; motifs par tons entiers, chromatismes et modalité ; trilles, *grupetto* et mordants

Teil 5 – Wiederholung aller bisher gelernten Tonarten; Ganzton- und chromatische Muster; Kirchentonarten; Triller, Doppelschläge und Mordente

113.

114.

115.

116.

117.

118.

119.

Scherzando

mf leggiero

f

120.

Valse

mf

p

mf

f

p

Modal Pieces.
Phrygian mode.

Pièces modales.
Mode phrygien.

Stücke in Kirchentonarten.
Phrygisch.

121.

Allegro moderato

mf

p

p

pp

p

mf

sub. p

mf

sempre mf

Mixolydian mode.   Mode mixolydien.   Mixolydisch.

122.

Alla marcia

Lydian mode.   Mode lydien.   Lydisch.

123.

Energico

Aeolian mode.   Mode éolien.   Äolisch.

124.

Tristamente

Dorian mode.   Mode dorien.   Dorisch.

125.

Pentatonic.   Pentatonique.   Pentatonisch.

126.

Phrygian mode.   Mode phrygien.   Phrygisch.

127.

Whole tone.   Ton entier.   Auf eine Ganztonleiter aufbauend.

128.

129.

130.

131.

132.

133.

134.

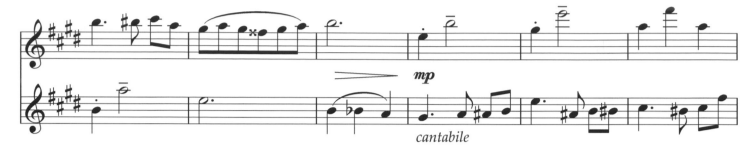

135.

136.

Adagio – dreamily

p mysterioso

pp poco agitato

rit. e dim.

137.

Allegretto

mf

f

mp

mf

f

mf

poco rit.

p

mf

p

mp

138.

Scherzando

139.

140.

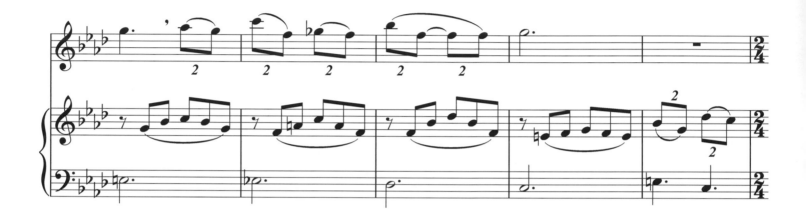

141.

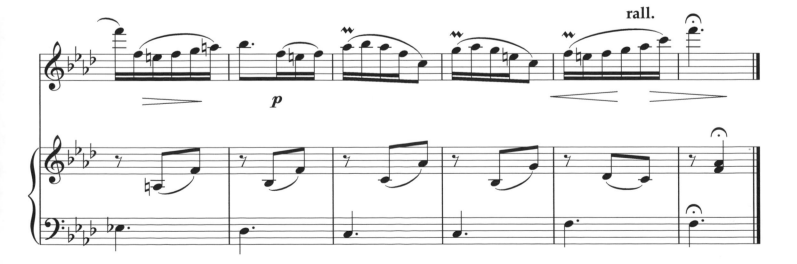

142.

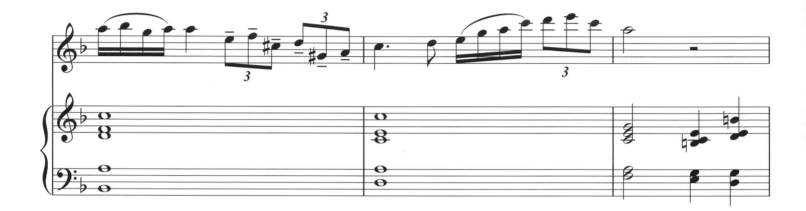

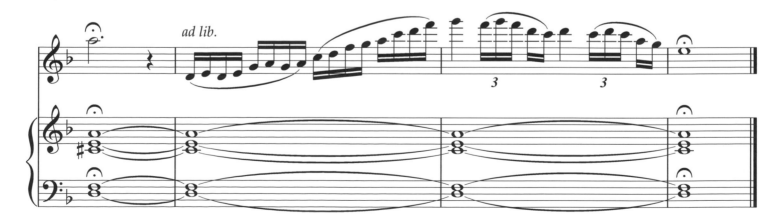